The Myopic's Vision

Virginia Lowe

The Myopic's Vision
A Poetic Memoir

To John, who has given me fifty years of joy
and, as a fellow poet, has read and commented on all the poems.

And to our two children –
we were honoured to share their childhood.

The Myopic's Vision: A Poetic Memoir
ISBN 978 1 76109 518 4
Copyright © text Virginia Lowe 2023
Cover image: Julien Meehem

First published 2023 by

GINNINDERRA PRESS
PO Box 3461 Port Adelaide 5015
www.ginninderrapress.com.au

Contents

1944 – Weeaproinah	9
1945 – Poem for Grandmothers	10
1946 – Words and Birds	14
1947 – The Past	15
1948 – Fluttering and Dancing	16
1949 – One December Day	18
1950 – Sex and the Soldier Beetle	19
1951 – Primary Vignettes	20
1952 – Forgetting How to Ride	27
1953 – Writing Progress	29
1954 – Republican Songs	31
1955 – Eucalyptus Christmas	37
1956 – Describing Tom	38
1957 – Cousins	39
1958 – Commitment?	41
1959 – *The Mill on the Floss* on the Tram	43
1960 – Burnt	45
1961 – Snake	47
1962 – Speech Night	48
1963 – Knowledge	50
1964 – Watercolour	52
1965 – Love the Oxymoron	53
1966 – The Company We Keep	54
1967 – Insomnia	56
1968 – Footsteps	57
1969 – Hello Yellow	59
1970 – Postcodes	60
1971 – First Child	62
1972 – Red Hardbacks	65
1973 – Mothering: Arachnids	67

1974 – Twenty-eight Boxes	68
1975 – Longed-for Second Child	70
1976 – Shades of Green	71
1977 – No Opinion Whatever	72
1978 – Mothering: Ekphrastic	73
1979 – Daddy! Daddy! The Sun's Come Up!	74
1980 – A Daughter Plays With Alice	75
1981 – Can You See the Brown Bear?	76
1982 – Moondance: Phillip Island	78
1983 – Mothering: Arboreal	80
1984 – Blue Stocking	81
1985 – A Spenser Fitte	82
1986 – *Aus Australien*	86
1987 – Eltham Retreat	90
1988 – Girda and the Robber Girl	92
1989 – The Juggling Librarian	96
1990 – Dilemmas of Spring	99
1991 – Go Gently	101
1992 – All Around my Hat	103
1993 – Monkey Mia	105
1994 – The Ages of Mankind	107
1995 – Conception of a Grandmother	111
1996 – Baby Grandchild	112
1997 – Our Front Door	115
1998 – Real People	117
1999 – Malaysia	120
2000 – Worlds: Creation and Demise	124
2001 – Open Heart	125
2002 – His Favourite Word	127
2003 – Palm Sunday	129
2004 – St Petersburg Animals	131
2005 – Grandfathers	134

2006 – For a Cat is Good to Think On	136
2007 – Dedication	138
2008 – Bianca	140
2009 – War Story	144
2010 – Everything Has Meaning	146
2011 – Break-fast	148
2012 – Land/Lord	149
2013 – Regrowth: Falls Creek (3 Haiku)	151
2014 – Jo's Farewell	152
2015 – Aylan Kurdi	155
2016 – The Truth is Out	156
2017 – Hair	158
2018 – Moonshadows	160
2019 – Thylacine	161
2020 – Old One Dicing (5 prose poems)	163
2021 – My Lockdown Life	168
2022 – Tree Skin	169
2023 – Smells	170
Acknowledgements	171

1944 – Weeaproinah

She first inspected it with
a brisk breeze urging
the bright cloud shadows
in their game of chasings
across fold upon fold of larkspur mountains

But now
through steamed-up windows
only low cloud is visible
wrapping the Otways in fog,
then lifting just high enough to fall as rain
flailing the house in fierce gusts

Eventually the stunning view returns
with high sky and gentle wind.
At last washing can be hung
nappies, sheets,
heavy despite the wringer,
fought with and pegged at last
to flap gaily in the breeze –
which turns to the familiar howling gale.
Sheets now horizontal
With a loose peg, a sheet is snatched
flying off towards the blue mountain range
She weeps tears of frustration

But the baby laughs and reaches,
catching the wind in her starfish hands
a love affair that will last a lifetime.

1945 – Poem for Grandmothers

after Margaret Atwood

Now I see us all as grandmothers
Actual or potential
Awaiting or experiencing
the infinite pleasure
of the small body in the arms
The simple giving and receiving
on which the first relationships
are based

>Baby warm
>Baby demanding
>Baby loving
>Baby living

So then I am forced to see
myself as grandchild
The first child of
the most loved daughter
Starved by routine
night-screaming
Feed the child!
you cried to deaf ears
Ears that knew
scientifically best
One day the grandmother's role
will be to sit by the fire
and nurse the infant

Not easy to bear in silence
when through your own five babies
you knew

Only grandparent
Sole representative of a race
to which I now belong
I did not understand
the love you must have felt
only resented
your sharpness, your dominance
your very presence, even

Though not at first
Milly Molly Mandy
read cuddled on your bed
and songs
'After the ball is over'
'I don't want to play in your yard'
'Daisy, Daisy'
These feel antediluvian
They represented for me
A time, a way of life
long gone, even then
A first belief in
the historical past

But now I see
they are only the equivalents
of what I sing
'All the pretty little horses'
'Summertime'
'Donna, Donna'
(All sad, all minor key
the mother notes)
Will they stand for him
as quaintly outdated
as belonging to an unimaginable past
a historical past
told of
but scarcely believed?

Grandma said
Look at my face –
So ugly, the wrinkles
At four I replied
What does it matter?
You'll be dead soon, anyway
Always at death's door
she lived another forty years

Will he, innocently callous
bring my mortality
home to me?
Or will the presence of
a great-grandmother
protect me
for a time?

I am not denied
the grandmother's role
It will be my life
my past
that gives him
his first tentative glance
at history

1946 – Words and Birds

A queue of curious pelicans
A cue of queueious pelicans
The English language
never ceases
to amaze
and amuse

Mother counted twenty-four
swans and pelicans
on Lake Colac once
when I was a child
in the days
when the lake
was full
before
climate
change
really
hit.

1947 – The Past

'The past is a foreign country' – Hartley

They do things differently there
as on Aunty Soph's gatepost

An old gnarled tree stump
covered with small smooth
porcelain figures
Asian – Chinese or Japanese
Houses, temples, tiny bridges too
A landscape, a tiny country
Bumpy hills and valleys
dotted with the little people
quaint, dressed in kimonos
fancy old-fashioned clothes.
Some men had lengthy beards
They were old
The miniature world enchanted me

Imagine Aunt setting it up
with patience and care
I would never disturb it
unless writing about it does?

1948 – Fluttering and Dancing

There is a piece of land
in Barramunga
in the remote Otway Ranges
where once a house
burnt to the ground
A chimney stands
and the remains
of a flower bed
Where bulbs had grown
unchecked unpicked
for more than a century

The bed of daffodils
had grown into an acre
and most of them
had a mutation
making them solid of trumpet
frilly of surrounding petals
But still of course
the definition of yellow

We sit down amongst them
and pick till our arms
can hold no more
You cannot even see
where we have been sitting
let alone where
the flowers have been taken
They are so close
so tightly packed
they fill the gaps
at once

The floor at the back
of the car
is filled to overflowing
with yellow

On return
ten years later
the acre of daffodils
is now an acre of potatoes
The beautiful mutations
no longer toss
and dance

The breeze is no longer sprightly
But then no more am I
seventy years later now
What wealth to a whole lifetime
Wordsworth and his daffodils!

1949 – One December Day

Little Friend Susan
had a swing in her backyard
Gently swinging you could see
over their strawberry patch
Swinging high you could look
into our backyard
and higher again, the street
I was allowed swing after swing
turn after turn
on a day in December
so I saw the green car pull up
in front of our house
Mum coming home at last
bringing my baby brother

1950 – Sex and the Soldier Beetle

Soldier beetles red and black
Swarmed around our coal shed door
Often marching back to back
We kids puzzled more and more
Why they marched about so oddly
We little knew of functions bod'ly
So, confused, were left to wonder
Why they should so rashly blunder

Who would choose to be pulled backwards
Powerless, without control
Follow where the other staggers
Half a pairing, never whole?

We little children knew our worth
Independent self-absorbed
The need to see where we would go
Assert our feelings, be ourselves.
Only grownups understood it
The beetles' pairing and denying

And they did not explain to children
That it was sex that soldier beetles
Presented on parade.

1951 – Primary Vignettes

Mystery

Mother dressed me in
grey tunic
white shirt
green tie
green bows on plaited hair –
A new teacher stopped me
What school did you go to before?
How could I answer?
Why would she even ask?
I've always been here
at Colac West State School.

Learning to Read

The cards are
long rectangles
of thick cardboard
corners worn round
All I can remember
is O for Orange
and the orange
is dull orange
Then *John and Betty*
followed by
The School Paper
The School Readers
Oh, the magic!

Injustice

After lunch
we stand in line
to walk back into class
and I am told off
for talking –
How to explain
that I am only
talking to myself
Whispering
The water is rising
It's coming closer and closer
having just listened
to the flood episode
of *Blue Hills*?

Time

Returning early
from piano
one spring morning –
the others still in class (RE)
a teacher working in the sun
asks me to check the time.
In the cool school corridor
I look at the big clock face
but all I can tell on return is
The little hand is past eleven
and the big hand is on two
Humiliation.

Snow

The day it snowed
we were let out to play
Amazed, ecstatic
When we came in
we were warned
not to warm our frozen hands
by the fire
in the corner grate
for fear of chilblains
But we did
anyway.

Drawing

In the playground
near the swings
a patch of dirt
and a stick –
I quickly sketch
a cup and saucer
competently large
One of the big girls
from her swing
notices and admires.

Pastels

We're told to draw
a rainy day with umbrellas
and not to go over it
with rain
but I disobey –
Diagonal white lines
almost cover all
and I am enchanted
with the
effect.

Boiled Lolly

Everyone
had an injection
this time
Even including me
After the jab
a boiled lolly from a bag
You could choose
But mine was horrible
worse than the sharp pain
the disappointment

Schoolyard

Shelter sheds
are for playing
What's the time, Mr Wolf?

Quadrangles
are where crates of morning milk
are stacked in the sun
and for Monday assembly

Flag Ceremony

Every Monday morning
assembly in the yard
We honour king and country
and the whole school sings
Australian sunsets
Are-stress-us —
Who knows
what any of it
means?

Houses

The sharp smell
of dry needles
under the big old pines
We girls
shape the outlines of walls –
bedroom, loungeroom, kitchen
bathroom, laundry, toilet –
And play houses
with a whole house
each.

Shop

The shop
next door to school
sold red iceblocks
in square cones –
which quickly got soggy –
for tuppence
Also gobstoppers
and sherbet bombs
and White Knights
But not often
to me.

Lying

Walking past school
I said to my mother
When I was a little girl
I used to kiss this fence.
Now I spit on it
It wasn't even true
I loved school
But it sounded
sophisticated

1952 – Forgetting How to Ride

My father loved the stars
In another life,
permitted education,
his facility with numbers
might have made him
a famous astronomer
instead of an accountant
See that bright one?
That's Beetle-juice
I remember him telling
Yes, I'd say meekly
wishing to please
But I couldn't of course
It was all just fuzzy blobs

See that milkbar on the corner?
No I said. Didn't want to be sent
somewhere I couldn't see
Stupid child! they thought
It never occurred to them
that I really couldn't see.

So on my seventh birthday
a bicycle purple painted,
with *Virginia*
in gold down the crossbar
the most beautiful bike ever seen
I was terrified to ride it

I couldn't see
where I was going
what was in front
I walked it to school
to Brownies after school
to have it admired,
to show it off
but I couldn't actually ride it.

Six months later my myopia
finally spotted by a teacher
I learned to ride
with my new glasses
I was never very good
never enthusiastic
never worthy of the bike's beauty
The skill now long forgotten

1953 – Writing Progress

At first it was slates
with squeaky slate pencils
and tied-on rags
to wipe them clean
But the rags weren't clean
Spat on too often
not often washed
they smelt vile

Pencils, lead pencils
came next
neatly whittled flat space
for your name
You turned the handle
on the big metal sharpener
importantly, out the front

Finally advanced to ink
Nibs and inkwells
The wells were sludgy
at the bottom
and at the top
sometimes inserted
by the class clown
the ends of some girl's plait

If you had been extra good
you got to be the ink monitor
for the week

The majestic progress
to fountain pen
not a minute too soon.

1954 – Republican Songs

1. Scraps of Royalty

I've got thirty-three
how many have you got?
I've got thirty-nine
and eight of them are coloured!
That green one – that's not coloured?
'Course it is – green's a colour!
But   But
it's only got one colour
That's like black and white…
Nah! Green's a colour!

She was winning
obviously
But the injustice of pasting
the green and white photo
from some magazine
(Pix?)
in the back
Counting it with
the much prized
coloured ones
rankles still today.

The making of
Royalty Scrapbooks
occupied much of our time
that year,
nineteen fifty-three.

Princess Elizabeth
soon to be crowned!
The glamour! The fervour!
Prince Philip was boring
No childhood at all
and he wasn't going to be king
not ever
Pictures of the Royal Wedding
Pictures of the happy mother
Pictures of Prince Charles
And little Princess Anne.

We knew the Coronation dress
had wattle for Australia
maple leaves for Canada
thistle for Scotland
embroidered all in gold
and real jewels.
We could recite the stones
in Edward the Confessor's crown
and the meaning
of the orb.

2. A Sickie

I was home from school
in bed with a cold
what luxury!
Books to read
hot chocolate to drink.
Wireless beside
to listen to
(though a big girl of nine)
Kindergarten of the Air.
Boys and girls come out to play
it started and
Good morning girls and boys
When
Oh no!
Queen Mary was dead!
Who cared?
She wasn't even
Princess Elizabeth's mum.
But to waste a whole day
with nothing on the wireless
but solemn music!
No story, no songs, no games
on *Kindergarten.*
No episode of *Blue Hills*
to listen to
with lunch.
It just wasn't fair

3. Swapcards

The pack of swapcards
lost tragically
on holiday in Sydney
at ten.
Two hundred or so
lovingly swapped,
or painstakingly chosen
Bought with pocket money
garnered from
iceblocks and licorice straps
musk sticks and sherbert bombs
had included
three of the Queen.
Their value was still high
though by now
I preferred
the real paintings
These were my specialty
Blue Boy and *Pinkie*
(Always a pair)
The Hay Wain
The Laughing Cavalier.
Photos,
even of the Royal Family
were not Art
I knew that.
But I grieved for those three
along with the others.

4. Justice

One day
There would be justice.
All would be revealed
There on our doorstep
Suddenly
Queen Elizabeth
Come to claim me
As her own daughter

Left a while
with her loyal
colonial subjects
JoyceAndNormanPaddle
who (illogically)
had no idea
I was really
a princess
Princess Virginia
Sister to
Prince Charles.
Then they'd be sorry!
But though I waited
patient through injustice –
through the stupidity
crassness
poverty
of my substitute parents,

substitute home
the one-storey playhouse
the unexciting school
the general lack
of glamour

Somehow I was
never claimed
and acclaimed
by my true mama.
No one knew
I was really a princess
until it was
too late.

And I wasn't a princess at all.
The glamour had gone.

I wouldn't be a princess now.
not if you paid me
all the
licorice allsorts
sherbert bombs
rainbow suckers
musk sticks
gob stoppers
chocolate freckles
White Knights
raspberry iceblocks
In the world!

So there.

1955 – Eucalyptus Christmas

A huge gum tree branch
propped in a corner of the room
touched the ceiling
Big enough to support
the actual gifts
for everyone invited to the party
Decorated with the presents,
ornaments, tinsel and balloons
specially, a month early,
for my birthday
It was satisfying
the balloons
the hanging gifts
so carefully chosen
so brightly wrapped
Like Dad's family Christmases –
the European small pine tradition
translated to the gigantic native

But Mother disapproved –
dropped leaves twigs
there in her best room
Besides originating with his family
a tradition not to be continued

So it only happened once
but it was glorious

1956 – Describing Tom

So how would you describe
Tom Sawyer?
he asked Grade Five.
I shot my hand up
taking pride in knowing
superstitious.
It came out as *suspicious*.
I don't think so he said scornfully
moving on to the mundane
attempts of others.
You'd think he'd have known
of my wide reading
so given me the benefit of the doubt
and help me find
the word I was aiming for.
Even *he* didn't propose
Superstitious

1957 – Cousins

Rough bark
comforting on palms and thighs
Fresh breeze
sprung up as darkness fell
Garden
at night, seen from high above
Hidden
My own place, my own dimension
Silent
listening as he calls my name

Wildness
and laughter have gone from his voice
Ceased now
giggling chases through Gran's house
Because
I have completely vanished
Now he
desperately wants to find me
Catch and hold

He's changed
It is no longer a game
He's sad

A noise
that reveals my presence
Now I
invincible in air
climb down
I go partway to meet him
halfway
In a lower fork
we meet

He pulls me roughly towards him
My face
is turned away
He turns it back

Let me
he says and tries a kiss
I say
I'm only eleven, no!
Too young
And anyway, we're cousins!

We trail
listlessly back inside the house
An event
that never happened
stands forever
between.

1958 – Commitment?

He was an older man
gauche, spotty, adolescent
Worse, brother of a non-friend
worse worse, ill-read
Sat by me or in front, behind
morning by morning
on the bus to school
I was flattered, confused,
embarrassed, tongue-tied

One morning he showed me
a ring – a keyring
with a reticulated
metal fish attached
Its sinuous movements
piscine and alluring
Fascinated, I praised it inordinately

As I shouldered my bag
at the station stop
he pressed it warmly
with a wink into my hand

Later mornings he seemed
to have established some claim
took the seat beside me as if by right

What did it mean
to have accepted a ring
from a man?

It lay leadenly, a guilty secret
hidden in the detritus
at the bottom of my school bag

I worried over weeks
Complicity? Commitment?
niggling at the back of my mind

Then one morning *Enough*
Missing a train
I ran back to the bridge
over Gardiner's Creek
took the captivating talisman
in my hand and flung!

Fish to water it sank
And I was free

1959 – *The Mill on the Floss* on the Tram

It's twenty years
since she left it on a tram
loved volume, loved offspring

Cheap binding
maroon cloth
war-poor paper
but covered
with youthful enthusiasm
and pink wallpaper
dotted with rosebuds

Read as a child
The mental picture of a mill pond
Maggie had a brother as did I
In their death they were not divided
no memory of the division before death
Romantic
Idealised sibling love
Idealised English landscape

Vivid now
the artefact, the book
Snatches from my childhood
Twenty, sixty years gone

Photos not taken
leave the most vivid images
Neither slides nor prints in the album,
not even screensavers
The moments unrecorded by camera
are the most clearly recorded by memory

And the books?
It's not those unread
But those read
and physically gone
The stories influence a life
The Mill on the Floss on the tram

1960 – Burnt

In primary school
a year is a lifetime
Being a grade above
made him older, wiser
infinitely attractive

This was not
mere adoration from afar
Providentially
our parents knew each other
his twin sister
was my friend
Family outings
were not infrequent

One summer Saturday
we took them to Mornington
All day together!
In a hired boat
he rowed me
– only me –
up and down
parallel to the beach
Then we lay on the sand
and talked

We three sat
in the back of the Holden
coming home
Me in the middle

The leatherette seat
stuck to my sweaty
raw burnt skin
so I slipped a hand
under my thigh
to ease the pain
And there
unseen by all
he took my hand in his.

All the way home
deeply uncomfortable
sunburn stinging
arm twisted
pins and needles imminent
I travelled
in rapture

1961 – Snake

after D.H. Lawrence

And I have something to expiate: a pettiness
How many times
in the years since school
has this phrase reverberated
when I have done something petty
or neglected a kindness

But not to do with a snake
Perhaps the phrase has lived with me
because I knew snakes –
knew snakes without fear
my brother's pets
Sinuous bright green Esmeralda tree snake
suitable to wear as a scarf draped round your neck
We could hold her, smooth sensuous scales,
but she constantly curved herself back towards him
Persephone the diamond python
growing larger and longer as she aged
dying at the grand old age of twenty-six
unheard of for a python

My pettiness concerns people not reptiles
I always seem to have something to expiate

1962 – Speech Night

December was hot
that final year
Several girls fainted
there on the oval
Some of the rest
wished we could

Afternoon after afternoon
the rehearsals continued
First everyone filing
through the imaginary
labyrinthine corridors
onto the imaginary stage
The oval's grass already
dry and worn

Then choir only
We reshuffled into
height order
Sopranos first
The ghosts of
future white dresses
swirling around us
or rather clung to our
sweaty bodies
ravaged by heat

But at last the night arrived
Our white dresses
invaded the elegant mysterious
wood-panelled corridors
behind the stage
of the Melbourne Town Hall

We took our places
as we'd been drilled
Listened respectfully
to Dr Wood
to the principal's principles
as it were
Sang a classy classical piece
then a school song
for the last time
tears running down
unchecked

1963 – Knowledge

The *four letter word*
I knew it existed
I knew what it meant
but had never
heard it said
seen it written –
Even asked directly
best girlfriend, boyfriend
could not bring themselves
to articulate it
in my presence –
Station graffiti
seeing me coming
must have dropped it
discreetly
from the walls

D.H. Lawrence I knew –
poetry first
'Snake' and others
then *Sons and Lovers*
so when at work
I was offered a copy
– still banned –
of *Lady Chatterley*

I accepted
with alacrity
and read his sensuous descriptions
with delight
(I was not, in point of fact
so very innocent)
And of course
discovered too
the Mysterious Word

My mother
poor prim innocent
would not have known
the Word
would not have even known
or so I thought
of its existence
But she did know
and roundly approved
of censorship –
She was horrified
for my morals
and even more
for my good name –
Not, so much
that I had read the book
but that – Oh shame! –
I had borrowed it
from a *MAN!*

1964 – Watercolour

Saffron and rose madder
sea-sheet reflects
in symmetry the sky
On this burnished brightness
waves encroach
Leaden opaque they flow
zinc white against
the watercolour's glow

A vision or a concept
beckons bright
But words
which seemed so clear and pure
across it spread
do nothing but obscure

1965 – Love the Oxymoron

'I turn round…I am in love' – Yeats
(Inspired by Liz Williams's sculpture *In Love*)

Stolid weighty unmoving
dizzying, round we go
Dog benign, pure white girl
knickers impurely on show
Balanced on four feet or two hands
destabilised, heels above head

Perfect girl, perfect St Bernard,
realistic, a fantasy act
Yeats around the skirt moves us
dumb beast implacable stands

Dizzying stolidity
innocent impurity
balanced instability
realistic fantasy

First love

1966 – The Company We Keep

After Wayne Booth

Well, in the library enshrined
we often feel ourselves alone.
But books are company, we find
or authors, when our minds are one.

No other mind communicates
directly with ours, as does this.
Another's thoughts are thought by us.
we do the work   mysterious,

We learn about another mind.
'Knowledge is power'. Surely true.
And knowledge of our humankind
is value even more to you.

A useful fact, the way to learn
to check a statement, not accept
the word of media mogul, or
prime minister, or cabinet

can give control of lives, of means
and ways to help a world in need,
But even more to empathise,
to go along with, as we read.

In prejudice, in pain, in grief,
'surprised by joy', alive, aware,
to feel the way that it must feel
to live in sunshine or despair.

This books will give you. You will be
a richer person. Laugh and weep.
We understand the author's mind
and know 'the company we keep'.

1967 – Insomnia

Lying awake
thoughts scurry like ants
whose activity seems random
only because we cannot perceive
their method of communication
or understand their underlying plan

Frenetic pest-like thoughts
randomness only apparent
Recognise their orderliness,
they are trying to tell you something
They are being thrown up for a reason

Thoughts that swarm like pests
can be herded into a poem

1968 – Footsteps

Step lightly on the earth they say
And I know one who will obey
Whose every step is straight erased
No harm, no influence, he craves
No power.

Each baby snail from greens removed
And carried out on fingertip
To eat again the silver beet
Instead of being cooked or killed
Attests this.

Cats abound, nurtured, indulged
Never dislodged from patient lap
Unless another human cries
Anyone's needs, but not his own
Attended.

Children too are never curbed
Restrained, no outside form imposed
His opinions kept from them
Their stepping-shaping barely felt
So gentle.

In chaos theory, pattern grows
Nurtured to its changing form;
Empowered individuals
Growing expanding wild and free
His triumph.

His life says See I was not here
I stepped as lightly as I could
I fell asleep to not converse
I barely touched the universe
Today.

But oddly this is power too.
A role filled in this selfless way
Enables, leaves the way to self
For others who can grow and say
See, here there is a footprint soft
And gentle, but discrete and formed
It makes the pattern, though it's light
And leaves creation better than
it was before.

1969 – Hello Yellow

No yards of tulle
No orange blossom
No tiara woven of flowers

No floor-length gown
No satin no lace
No train or bearer

Not ivory or white
though silk it was
Sunny yellow
Mini skirted

A floppy straw hat
impossibly wide
in yellow
No coy veil

A non-princess dress
on a day far too important
for playing dress-ups
Symbolising practicality
Portending happiness and contentment
for forty-seven years
with a beautiful partner

1970 – Postcodes

Our marriage two weeks old
a small, rather grotty flat
2795 Bathurst –
Postcodes had only just come in
a new idea, and fascinating

Wahroonga 2076
That's where I used to live!
Uh huh I reply
Where was it you were born?
Colac, that's right! That's 3250

After a suitable interval
I sigh deeply
He is instantly beside me
with a consoling cuddle
What is it darling?
I hate doing dishes!
Poor darling!

Full of sympathy
he returns to his codes
Bega is 2550
I have an uncle who lives there!
I've reached the drying stage
and sigh again
Another cuddle
We'll get a dishwasher
just as soon as we have a house
he promises

Coober Pedy 5723
It sounds so romantic!
I'm scouring the benches now
Another sigh, another cuddle
Ah romance

We sit across the table
over shining mugs of coffee
The kitchen sparkles
They say you should tell
when you are upset
Instant concern

Oh dear, Darling
what's the matter?

I'd have loved a hand
with the dishes

Well…
why didn't you drop me a hint?

1971 – First Child

Sixteen years ago
you made me a mother
I sat up and watched you emerge
crying healthily –
auburn fuzz, squashed nose,

The given name I thought
was of startling originality
of Victorian aunts
romantic heroines
(Scott's *Ivanhoe,*
Sharp, Thatcher)
A mixed bunch
purely literary
No one, no one anyone knew
was ever actually called that

Auburn fuzz replaced
by thick golden curls
The original name
turned out to be quotidian
So many of them
never less than two
in her class at school

Without a distinctive name
or titian hair;
the individuality
the originality –
what the hair
and the name
had meant to me –
are there
embodied
in a blond sixteen-year old
of intelligence, wit,
creativity
strength
and individuality.

Perhaps a name
not yours alone
encourages the mind.

You can't rely
on name alone
for individuality
That must be worked for,
worked at
Individuality
personality
not granted,
with a distinctive name.

So you create
an individuality
strong and all your own;
And you give it names,
distinctive, unusual,
shared with characters
you loved

Piglet, Sniff
Snufkin, Dickon
Hypatia…

One day you will
find a name
that fits exactly
and all your own.

1972 – Red Hardbacks

On my tenth birthday
best present ever
bound in red
The Australian Encyclopaedia
Ten volumes
packed neatly in a box
I'll never forget the smell
the thrill

Replaced as most prized
by another
in red solid covers
big, foolscap
and not even printed
My sloppy speedy handwriting
Volume twenty-one
nineteen seventy-eight
February to
July

The Reading Journal
no longer in scrappy
ephemeral exercise books
Finally treated with respect
Solid, enduring
To record the responses
Of our two children
and more and more
as they grew
wiser

Six thousand
handwritten pages
in twenty-six volumes
Completely irreplaceable
My favourite possession
A labour of love
or just plain craziness
The Reading Journal
of books we read
to both children
from birth to eight
Their responses
meticulously detailed
Indexed under author
and theme
Blue ink for first child
red for second
Now delightful thoughtful
adults

A reminder to
never underestimate –
development of mind
enshrined

1973 – Mothering: Arachnids

Oh look! I cried
to the high-chaired child
feigning delight

I fetched a glass
and some paper thin
For the very first time
as brave as a lion
I trapped one

I think it would prefer
to be outside
I told the child

Leaving lunch
together we scanned
the garden and she
carefully chose a bush
Pretty flower she said

So I let it go onto a leaf

I am a mother
doing
what mothers do

1974 – Twenty-eight Boxes

John had already left
for his new job in Melbourne.
I waited with the toddler
and my parents
in the empty house.
Everything packed
and ready to go
Food, nappies
Nothing was left

A moving van
pulls up outside
Driven five hundred miles
from Melbourne
and overnighted
somewhere I presume
Right on time, but so small

Two jolly giants bounce in
ready to begin
Their faces dropped
as they surveyed
our possessions
They could clearly see
that as we feared
the furniture, the crockery
clothing and ornaments
just would not fit

Turned away shaking their heads
We knew no one could have
that many books!
Clearly it was a mistake!
But John, a college librarian
had just moved his library
to a new building
he knew exactly
and had filled it out
on the form

Two double beds
One sofa, one dining table
one cot, one washing machine
So it went on
And our two book collections
together made up
the twenty-eight boxfuls

Crestfallen
they set off back to Melbourne
to return two days later
with a larger van
While we set to unpacking
the bedding, the food
the nappies
To survive living
another two days
in a packed-up house.

1975 – Longed-for Second Child

One strong startled cry
as the open mouth
the sticky black curls
encounter air
for the first time

A beautiful little person
the father's genes and mine
started with love
grown to meet
the love that is waiting

1976 – Shades of Green

Cocooned in greenness
our house holds its coolness
Different shapes of leaves
through every window
Huge monstera
with Emmental holes
Banana leaves which grow
towards the roof
while you look away
Fig leaves hide figs
Hibiscus leaves expose flowers

Myriad shades of green
through every window
Grape leaves adorn the pergola
shade the sunroom
Golden elm's yellow-green
shades the roof
The passionfruit vine
forms blinds half drawn
across a top window
In summer

In winter
most lose their leaves
letting in sun and warmth

While the climate heats
nature's air-con survives
and we stay cool
in our house of nearly
fifty years and counting

1977 – No Opinion Whatever

She sat before the fire
She sat beside the cat
Addressed the beloved moggie
with inappropriate
appropriated
words

'Lll.' I can say 'lll.'
When I was a little girl
I had no opinion whatever of lll
and it was true
she could now pronounce
'lib'ry' instead of 'yib'ry'
I took a tremendous jump
off the top of the wall
and landed on the top of the cat

Fortunately her stories
were recited not performed
The cat never knew
what had almost hit him
and curled-slept on – despite
Beatrix Potter and *Benjamin Bunny*

1978 – Mothering: Ekphrastic

Botticelli: *Birth of Venus*

Ah to be
compared with Venus
Flattering
perhaps

Botticelli's *Venus*
admired by all
those painted flying
those mortal standing
in the Uffizi, Florence

Rising from the waves
she stands upon
her fluted shell
Rich curling hair
flying free
One hand modestly
cupped
Breasts smooth
and inviting

Toddler on my hip
takes one glance
Tries to hoik up
my sweater
shouting joyously
Breast-y!

I am a mother
refusing to do
what mothers do
(for now, anyway)

1979 – Daddy! Daddy! The Sun's Come Up!

We strange humans are capable of believing
two contradictory things at once.
In the dark and cold of a winter's two a.m.
confronted with a distressed two-year-old
All I could think of as I took her back to her cot
was: *You mustn't get up till the sun comes up!*
The next we heard was this joyous shout
to Daddy making breakfast in the kitchen
expressing: All's right with the world.
Daddy Daddy! The sun's come up! Mummy said it would!

The distress hadn't been about the dark or cold
but because she couldn't escape
from her ancient wicker cot
with all of her surprise morning books.
She clutched only two of the three
which she insisted be read in the big bed
before she and I got up to start the day.
We hadn't even known she could climb out
let alone lugging books as well.

Galileo's discovery that the Earth circles the Sun
I knew of course; and could even have
explained simply to Daughter, with the help
of an apple and a desk lamp
but not in the very middle of winter's night

1980 – A Daughter Plays With Alice

I'm the Cheshire Cat she says and grins.
Look! You've gone and spoilt my nice new rattle!
Sharpen your battle stick she cries and wins;
As Tweedledum, this daughter's fought her battle.
I don't believe in you she tells her friend
Who looks at her askance and laughs a bit.
And what if we are in a dream, then end?
Young friend does not appreciate her wit.
As Unicorn and Child imaginary
Bargain to believe they both exist,
The Queen and Knight in red are truly wary,
But still this crazy chess game will persist.
Thus logic and the language twists of hers
Engross both linguists and philosophers.

1981 – Can You See the Brown Bear?

Read-maker
The forgotten word
creates
the neologism
as does the whiff
of condescension

Author –
you who make
what I read –
Read-maker

A'course I can
the child says
Your question, author
rhetorical to you
is direct for me
the listener –
directed to me
by the text
and its mediator
reader-parent
interpreter –
also by you
the author

Read-maker
The neologism creates
the account of the moment –
This poem

Mediator,
parent-observer
writerly, writes
read-maker, I

I make of this word
words of my own
a pastiche
Reused words
spoken

and taken
onto paper –
Then spoken again

Can you see the brown bear?
A'course I can, Read-maker!

1982 – Moondance: Phillip Island

There it is
just ahead of me.
I can't catch it.
One foot can touch it –
breaking it into shards –
but there is no way
to jump on it.
It remains ahead –
a guide
or a chimera.

I'll let you have it
I say
and step back –
It is still with me
just ahead.
I look up.
He is doing it too –
this odd moondance.
trying to step on it,
to capture it.
He has
but can't hold –
one of his own.

If I catch him up –
if we stand together –
only then
can we share
the moon's reflection.
I can't think of anyone
I'd rather share
my moon with.

1983 – Mothering: Arboreal

Help!
The elder child's voice
rang from a tall pine
An excellent climber
fiercely independent
never called for help

With some anxiety
I peered up
Yes, there she was
right at the top
but followed
by her little sibling
who was blocking
her route down

Girding up my long
seersucker skirts
I took off after them
Reaching the younger
I guided them down
elder following

Thank goodness
It never leaves you
The ability to climb –
like writing a poem

I am a mother
who climbs and creates

1984 – Blue Stocking

I am the last of my species
Left without tertiary education
We can't afford to send two to uni
(though my brother was five years younger)
He'll have to support a wife and children

But I knew really
It was the blue stocking effect
Who'd want to marry
A girl with her head in a book
All the time?

I did find someone
Or he found me
A fellow librarian
All he wanted was a girl
With her head buried in a book
Who wanted to study, too

He even made passes
At a girl wearing glasses

Try to explain Blue Stocking
To a Millennial
Complete lack of understanding
A species fortunately extinct
Left behind by evolution

Eventually I became a mature student
a lecturer too
But now with a doctorate in hand

1985 – A Spenser Fitte

Contayning
The Legends of the Mature Aged
Mum at Monash
or
Of Exhaustion

A portrait of a common type
Of student here reveals
There's more to her than meets the eye
'Tis chaos she conceals.

1

A gentle student pricking o'er a book   *nail biting*
    One of an army[1] of right pleasant Dames
    That sit in front three rows[2] the board to look
    And lecturers disrupt far from their aims,[3]
    And questions ask, disturbing tutors' games[4]
    Aged thirty-nine about, or so they seem,
    Hair greying, harassed, glasses with thick frames,
    Earnest, well-read, voluble, they scheme
To survive the evening meal[5] ere running out of steam.

2

A Spenser essay: mere two thousand words   *excessive*
    Due Monday next. When will she ever learn?
    The Faerie Queene, a virgin (good for her:
    A queen needs not her daily bread to earn,
    Nor offspring organise, both calm and stern).
    A neverending epic,[6] all in rhyme
    (I've passed the creche![7] taken a wrong turn!)
    Duessa's[8] lust: where does she find the time?
The pity is that plagiarism's now a crime.[9]

3

A multitude of babes[10] about her hung,
    Playing their sports that joyed her to behold.
    If only they were not so weak and young,
    They could get tea themselves, have something cold,
    While she could study hard. She's feeling old.
    With time, she'd be a paragon of wit,
    But sausages to cook,[11] school problems told.[12]
    Bath children? Or read another crit?
At two a.m. to bed, the essay almost writ.   *after maelstrom*

4

'Her scattered brood, soon as their parent dear
>   They saw so rudely falling to the ground...'[13]
>   She knows how Errour feels, with kids to rear

infant goats

Ah yes, this has a most familiar sound!   *cacophony*
'Gathered themselves about her body round...
And sucked up their dying mother's blood.'
They're[14] certainly demanding, she has found:
No matter how one tries to do them good
Confusion reigns supreme,[15] as in the wandering wood.[16]

Acrasia Student

Notes

1. The 'army' indicates the gallant, but occasionally aggressive attitude of this group.
2. It has been pointed out that the typical position of the 'Dames' in lecture theatres is caused by the fact that they are notoriously weak of either sight or hearing, not necessarily by their being ingratiating toward the lecturers.
3. This assumes that every lecture does actually have an 'aim'. Alternatively, it can be taken to mean that the Dames do not 'aim' to disrupt lectures.
4. That is, carefully manipulated lesson plans for tutorials.
5. This 'meal' is extended in stanza 3, line 7.
6. This is what is known as 'poetic licence'. It is not an epic, but a mediaeval poetic allegory.
7. That is, she is so involved in thoughts of the imminent essay, while driving away from Monash, that she misses her way absentmindedly.
8. Duessa is the female villain of the piece. She is usually seen as representing duplicity, but 'lust' is also appropriate.

9. That is, she would take the easy way out by purchasing a pre-loved Distinction essay from a third year Honours student she knows.
10. A.S. has neglected to correct the inconsistency between the 'babes' and 'aged thirty-nine' in stanza 1, line 6, which implies much older progeny.
11. Food for thought, pre packaged for regurgitation.
12. An ambiguous phrase, usually interpreted as one of her children telling her about interactional conflicts at an educational institution.
13. Stanza 4 is essentially a dialogue between Spenser's text (in inverted commas) and the stream of consciousness it evokes in the Dame.
14. That is, her own offspring.
15. Presumably confusion reigns only in the home, not in her university activities. Anyway we hope so, and wish her all the best with the essay!
16. With apologies to Edmund Spenser's *Faerie Queene* and to *Pale Fire* by Vladimir Nabokov. V.L.

1986 – *Aus Australien*

In a church market square
In the heart of a town
In the heart of Germany
Sits a tiny pot
With a tiny plant
With one single flower
I bend and inhale
The sharp spicy odour
The stallholder
Watches my ecstasy
With wary curiosity
Lantana!
I explain joyously
But she knows that
The plant is labelled
Meticulously
So I try again
All but inarticulate
Aus Australien, Australien
She understands, nods
And shrugs benignly

She cannot see with me
The rampant weed
Covering Queensland acres
Or even the solid bushes
In almost every garden
In Victoria, at home

Still in Germany
A pet shop
Where a big white cocky
Sits dispirited
In its too small cage
We stare through the window
Delight and grief mixed
Then again desperately
Look for someone to explain to
Aus Australien…
Nobody cares
Nobody shares our vision
Flocks of sulphur-crested cockatoos
Wheeling over the fields
Decorating dead trees
Shouting in jubilation

In Ostia outside Rome
Homesickness reaches its height
Eucalypts, a whole forest
The scent of home
Flowing across the caravan park
In waves of nostalgia
One of the ubiquitous
German tourists asks
Where are those trees from?
Aus Australien

Another chips in
I thought Greek?
Nein, nein emphatically
Aus Australien
We're from Australia too
To establish our credentials
They smile politely
But cannot comprehend
Our delight

For a daughter it is different
Far from Europe
Suddenly discovered
Something glorious and homely
Symbolic and ordinary
Through a train window
In Zambia
To remind one of home

But as well there are
People who are fascinated
When pointed out
Europeans for whom it is
A thing of romance
Read about, dreamed of
And never seen before

And they are gripped
By stories
Of sharp cold clear nights
In the Wimmera
Or the dimmer glimpses
From the front yard at home
Where even the bright pall
Of city electricity
Cannot hide its design

The Southern Cross
And friends to share it with

1987 – Eltham Retreat

Cloistered
Almost five days
Between speaking to another person
Face to face.
This to me a retreat
Is to you a home
Of activity
Quiet but busy;
Friends and children
Come and go.

I hear
The mournful cry
Of the plover at night;
Rooster-crow as I watch
Dawn breaking,
Then punctuating the day
As the old clock's striking
Does.

The expanse of sky;
I watch rain showers
And tall clouds
Sweep over hills
Clad in trees.

The lush grassy
Bird-mountains
Of the yard,
Where blackbirds, thrushes and doves
Cavort.

Busy activity of birds
The only life visible
Except for a visit
From next-door's Alsatian
(She obviously
Found it very dull
Only thrushes and doves
To chase
And soon
Took herself off).

But I live.
And I write
A thesis on women poets.
So I also write
A poem for my daughter
And a poem for you, Soph
In gratitude
For the solitude
You have granted me
In the generous lending
Of your home

1988 – Girda and the Robber Girl

For Isobelle Carmody, with thanks to Hans Andersen's
The Snow Queen

1.

Girda and the Robber Girl
made an alliance
Using threats of violence
Using control of animals.
Through love or strength
they both found freedom
The independence they craved –
the Robber Girl
Alone with her pistols
Girda with her Kay.

Endings, you say
are difficult, and must be right,
Sometimes they glow
with rightness
and lift the hair
on the back of the neck
and leave all the possibilities
all the future
glowing ahead.

Holding hands
Girda and Kay
return home
to grandmother
with her Bible
and to their future
together.

2.

This is becoming allegorical
in ways I had not planned.
Are you really the Robber Girl
fierce and independent
and thoughtless, even cruel?
No, that's not fair
but the drama is there.

And I
Am I only a device
constructed by the pattern
to rescue the man
I love?

3.

The Snow Queen
is a story about sight
and distorted sight –
Which is the world?
Do myopic people
always see more clearly
because they know
that what you see
all depends
on where you stand?

What they perceive
without their glasses
is different
from everyone else –
They know
that the world is provisional only
varying for each person
The reality they live inside.

Who says
after all
what is distorted?
what is real?
Think about the eyes of a bee
or a cat
Is their reality any less real
because it is not the same as mine?

4.

Patterns –
a jigsaw of ice
It must be right
it must make the word
Eternity

The bounty of the universe
can be reduced
to a single word –
or perhaps a single
word-pattern.

Are all my patterns verbal –
verbal jigsaws?

5.

To return to the ending –
The romantic variety
says nothing
Leaves it all
to the hair
on the back of the neck
and the feeling of pattern
complete yet ongoing
as is the world
and the universe
However it is seen.

1989 – The Juggling Librarian

Well, in the library
Lunchtime Extravaganzas
you haven't seen
a performing librarian –
juggling, trapeze acts,
bareback riding.
You're right –
you haven't missed out.

You may, of course,
have seen a real
professional performing librarian
storytelling
to a spellbound crowd.

Believe it or not, however,
juggling
is an essential part
of the librarian's
bag of tricks
(alias professional expertise).

Take today
how to juggle writing the budget
(the computer down again)
while the creative muse
waits to strike
with a magazine contribution?

How to juggle
the earnest silent atmosphere
of Year 12 study
(there were certainly one or two
needing this
a week ago last Wednesday
I think it was?)
with the exuberance
of a Year 8 class
researching endangered animals
with enthusiasm?

Juggling
'the library as the place to be'
with
'reserved for just the VCE'

Juggling
the Year 9 child who needs advice
on what can possibly
reach the heights of
The Long Dark Teatime of the Soul
with the Year 11 adolescent
researching
possum trapping in the upper reaches
of the Murrumbidgee
1880s, please?

What type of computer program
do we automate with?
with
have we sufficient
picture books of dragons?

Helping staff devise
a Year 7 science assignment
with
blowing up balloons
for the forthcoming
Library Extravaganza.

The Juggling Librarian
not a myth
not a chimera
but here, now.
Come and view her
today…

1990 – Dilemmas of Spring

'When the hounds of spring are on winter's traces…' – Swinburne

Spring is sprung
So off to the back of the wardrobe
to dig out the lighter clothes there.

But dilemma strikes. Since last summer
a new awareness, a new responsibility
Step lightly on the Earth (Suzuki says)
All clothes should last at least five years

Fine. Most of my clothes are easily that age
But stockings!

Winter is no problem – bright warm ribs
– even if synthetic – look good, and with care
and judicious subtle mending last out five useful years

But nylons! The archetypal throwaway
A bare two days if you're lucky
Pollution-producing in their manufacture
and their disposal – such waste!

If it's as warm as that – why not bare legs?
Dilemma number two
To shave or not to shave, that is the question.

The feminist would advocate
that any job worth holding down
any person worth cultivating
would at best approve at worst ignore nature's fur.

Will we wax? (Excruciating)
Buy one of those expensive rippersoutbytheroots?
(Even more excruciating)
Depilate with toxic chemicals? Woe skin, environment
Bleach? Only if you can use something
ecologically sound – lemon juice perhaps?
Or the slings and arrows – no! nicks and rashes
of outrageous razors (non-disposable of course)
The most unkindest cut of all?

Perhaps back to the wimpish
half-hearted stance of former years
Ideologically sound, solid as a rock
underarms (and a penchant for short sleeves
rather than sleeveless!) *Piker! Coward!*
Decisions decisions. Oh bother the hounds of spring!

1991 – Go Gently

We killed him
my brother and I
Our kindly physician must have known
that the morphine
would be deadly to a body
that had known no medicine
had relied on God for healing
for over eighty years

We took it in turns
to sit by the bedside
my brother, my mother and I
I hope he realised
that the busts of laughter
from the living room
were an expression of our
communal nervousness
in the presence of immanent death
The children's partners
the grandchildren
waiting

The last sense to go
is hearing
We gathered round
turned up the sound
no flies buzzed
but a hymn
filled the room
He believed
he was prepared
to meet the Maker
he had served
faithfully
for so many years

1992 – All Around my Hat

'All around my hat
I will wear the green willow…' – sung by Steeleye Span

In a passionate burst of movement
Spontaneous, alive
One young man
Links arms with another
And they fling each other round
Stamping
With joy
To the old ballad
(Child 135?)
With its modern tune.

They are indescribably beautiful.

The others
Beautiful youths and maidens
(Pause for
completely
non-pejorative
irony)
Watch
Laugh
Interrupt their conversations –
Allusive
Comic
Earnest
Game talk
Merging into
Life talk

Politics talk
Relationships talk –
To join in the song
Raucously
Enthusiastically.

He's a poor deluded young man,
Let him go –
Farewell he!

I chop a mound of carrots
And grin with delight
They are here
I am here.

1993 – Monkey Mia

Word runs round the campsite
They're in! They're coming in!
Instantly the baking beach is crowded
We stand knee-high in sea
Yearning, stretching towards the horizon
Where the dolphins appear

A meeting, we trust, of minds
Eager as ours, for contact
For reaching across the species barrier
In love

They nudge our legs
We stroke their satiny sides
Well away from the eyes and
        blowhole vents
Each name age and relationship
Is learned from the dorsal fin
Distinctive, notched or bent
This is the larger part of the pod
Females and young

In supreme trust one mother
Allows her baby to come closer
Guarded and shepherded by its
        big sister
To swim between the legs
Right at the shore
Oh little one! we greet it
With rapture

They leave
The beach is deserted, desolate
Under the searing sun,
the blusterous hot wind

We leave
Drive back through the bright jewels
Strung on their breathless chain of heat –
Stromatolites and Pinnacles aeons old
A gorge and its curving
Stone-carving river –
There is a snake, a lizard
And woe! a car-slaughtered emu
Leaving its lifelong partner
Disconsolate

Back in Perth a small news item –
The dolphin baby is dead
Killed, it seems, by effluent from the camp
Oh little one!
It was our shit that was your doom

Home again
We bear bright cameos
Of beauty and strangeness and difference
Of wildness and creatures who trust
Of encounters with alien minds
Paid for by us with guilt and grief
Paid for by them with their lives.

1994 – The Ages of Mankind

'The silver race replaced the gold,
   inferior, yet in worth
Above the tawny bronze' – Ovid

She woke
to the liquid cry
of a bright-eyed currawong
staring down at her
and shouting
from the edge of her
tarpaulin roof
Breakfast time
You'd think that
alone on a platform
fifteen metres up a tree
you'd at least be able
to sleep in.

She had dreamt
of a world
where everyone
lived in trees
together or alone.
And the world
offered its bounty –
blackberries
yams honey
clear moss-filtered water –
and the trees

in their magnificence
were allowed to stand
tall there in their forests.
And people
were at peace.
A Golden Age.

She sighed
turned over
and sat up
to start breakfast
on her little stove
for currawong
and herself –
oaten porridge
with a few sultanas
honey, soy powder
She thought,
if the dream was Golden
I in this moment
am in the Silver Age.
I am at peace
with my environment.
I eat grain
cultivated by people
and brought to me
through the forest
on the backs of friends.

Possums and currawongs
feel no fear
unhunted, unharmed
They accept me
as part of the tree
and appreciate
the exotic crumbs
crusts and cores
I leave for them.
Here there is
heat and cold
rather than
golden eternal spring,
but I glory
in the changes
these bring.

And below me there
the world, the real world —
it is not even Brass —
it is not just warfare
it is devoted to
It is greed
stupidity evil
and unthinking
destruction.

The bulldozers roar
the men shout
Another day has begun
making bare
her forest
in a hard
Age of Iron.

1995 – Conception of a Grandmother

'Bless what there is for being' – Auden

Grandchild

A tiny creature floats
contained, content
in whose nascent mind
inheres a world in which
its mother's childhood
has no place
will not exist –

A world so real
so tangible to me
to this little one will be
forever mythical

Daughter

It was you
who made me a mother
who changed my life
by vesting me
with the mantle
of motherhood
You are mother-maker

But now
the world shifts
You are mother yourself
You bear within you
your own mother-maker

Mother-maker, you
and now child-bearer too

1996 – Baby Grandchild

Sense and Sensibility

The closing of the eyes in sleep
is a woeful business
What will I miss?
How do I know that the world
inexplicably occluded
still exists?

Even worse
is the wilful imposition
of stillness and darkness
by another

So my medium
rocks and pats
sings soothingly
all the while
unbeknownst to me
absorbed in Jane Austen

Baby Walking

While mangoes fall
in the intense northern heat
a baby, much too small
stands stolidly erect
then deliberately
loses balance
to step forwards
into his future
as a biped
And I am not there
to see

Encounter

They met at the back door
He was going out
she was coming in
Bemused enchanted
They stood face to face
eye to eye
She was charmed by
his long fluttering eyelashes
So she took a peck

Only eight months old
though already walking
Who was he to stand
between a chook
and her beloved
cat food?

1997 – Our Front Door

It's hard to find
our front door
A crazy brick path
through the trees – tall
and bushes – small
Random clumps of flowers
from tiny shy violets
to raucous orange clivea
There's the pear tree
the quince tree
Lebanese cress
strawberry guava
and feijoa trees
are the edible ones
The leaves are all different
Monstera huge
with Swiss-cheese holes
golden elm leaves
with lacy beetle holes
spider plant
pale green and white
ribbon-y spider legs
The huge green leaf-flowers
of the succulent aeonium
sometimes sporting
its yellow real-flower cones

All overgrown of course
but it keeps us cool
and unflustered in summer
and ensures that
each window and door
has a different-shaped leaf
to frame.

The door often stands open
if anyone can find it
for the cats' easy access
Few guests and none
are now welcomed in
few burglars and none are armed
Coronavirus is armed
fresh air has protected us
and has isolated us
So our front door is open

1998 – Real People

A one-year-old explores the world

Back and forth
Back and forth
He sweeps
Across the window
Of my mind
A small figure
Running earnestly
Pushing before it
A red broom
Just his height
Sweeping the kitchen floor

Autumn
The front porch
Covered in leaves
Here at last
Is a task
And a tool
Within his ken
The yard broom
Twice, three times his height
Collects
A satisfying pile
Of rustling leaves
Over the edge
He sweeps them
But cannot manipulate
The broom's head
Up again

With a tablespoon
From a huge mixing bowl
He feeds his Johnpa
As he is usually fed
From a bunnykins bowl
With a teaspoon

The new Iris Murdoch
Purloined
From the coffee table
Is read
On his own small sofa
Deep in concentration
He turns the pages

Playing quietly
At Johnpa's feet
Suddenly he jumps up
Heads for the laundry
And returns
Nappy in hand
To a spot
On the carpet
Presses then wipes
Vigorously
Yes, he has wet the floor
But he has also
Mopped it up

Once he has mastered
Getting onto
The kitchen chairs
His highchair
Decreases in importance
It is reduced
To part of a climbing frame
(kitchen chair to table
to highchair tray to seat)
No longer
A place to eat
Real people eat
At the table
On kitchen chairs

Toys?
What do people
Do with toys?
They collect them
And put them
Into containers
So, so do I
Over and over again

How do adults behave?
What do real people do?
Well look – I can do it too

1999 – Malaysia

Penang Morning

Already beads of sweat
Hang, catch the sun, then drip –
The purpose of eyelashes!

Roadways

Yesterday the river-road
by river-bus –
bathing buffalo
kingfishers
over-towering forest walls –
trees and shrubs bound by liana –
all vivid green –
Our outboard motor
the only disturbance –
River Tembling.

Today, the teeming human-road –
buses, cars, rickshaws
bikes both pedalled and motored,
share the road
with pedestrians
precariously –
Deep wide gutters spanned by steps
arcade shops open to the street
food vendors vending –
Myriad smells, human noise –
the ever-teeming life
of an Asian city street –
Penang.

Twilight

The twilit
forest path
beckons

He sets off
clad only in shoes
negotiating roots
selecting specific leaves
studying ants
confidently exploring

Moving outward
as the forest night
falls

Jungle Encounters

On the Track
A glimpsed monkey –
light brown, gibbon-sized –
several squirrels
large and small
(or tree-shrews?)

Ants in orderly columns
marching through the jungle
ten abreast along their road
of leaf and twig and branch
and track –
More than one species
is on the move today

And the constant sound
of bird and insect chorus.

In the Hide
Two bats dance together
about our heads and beds –
rat-friend, long tail, large eyes
(not *ratus ratus!*)
helps itself to food –
(boiled-egg shells
yield tasty scraps to gnaw –
a distinctive sound in the dark)
We jump at the deep bark
of the bullfrog in the water tank
but only the first time
From the window our torchlight
captures a deer
while the fireflies
continue to signal.

At the Jetty
Close to its body
a deep reddish blue,
then brilliant cornflower
with tiny white spots –
Almost a hand-width across
the butterfly
lands on hands
on hair and clothes –
Remains with us
throughout the wait
for the river ferry.

2000 – Worlds: Creation and Demise

A world is born
I sit and sing

Into this nascent world I bring
security and comfort
lullabies and nursery rhymes
human presence
in the earliest hours
of world-creation

By the humidicrib
I sit and sing

I sit and sing
in intensive care

comfort and love
hymns familiar and consoling
as a world ends

Her rich world –
> great-grandchild
> baby of delight
> late husband, sisters, mother
> houses, clothes, music
> elegant old furniture
> righteous indignation
> impulsiveness
> joy
> life experiences

that perspective ceases.

I sit and sing

2001 – Open Heart

What a great idea
I thought
before I could think clearly,
as they stuck
a transparent bandage-patch
over one of the various holes
that dotted my chest.
A window in the chest
I thought,
so they can check
on the heart
and watch
its mechanical valve
ticking away.

A window on the heart
Tristram Shandy decided
following the beliefs
of an ancient philosopher –
a window on the heart
would show at once
the character,
the sympathy, the humanity,
the moral rectitude
of the heart's owner.
None could be deceived.
The heart would show openly
the truth.

What a stupid idea
I thought
when I could think clearly again –
who can see through flesh
however marred,
however split and zippered up again?

But the moment's conviction
remained, because
even without
words or emotions
the literary allusion
sticks like a bandage –
and because
moral rectitude
is in very short supply.

2002 – His Favourite Word

My lover has a favourite word
It is *perpetrator*

I was slowly recovering
from a close encounter
of the inevitable kind

Ever by my hospital bed
I asked him
what had happened in the world
There was no good news
in the paper.

For many years
I had faithfully followed
For Better or for Worse
Lynn Johnston my guide
to parenting

The last strip I recalled
in their front yard
the father's model railway
had been vandalised
*Have they found
The perpetrator?*
I asked

After six weeks
no one knew
what had caused
the heart failure
the perpetrator unclear
here as well
nor if the valve repair
had saved my mind
as well as my heart

His favourite word
has lasted sixteen years

2003 – Palm Sunday

for the refugees

Nostalgically we march
with a child again –
a grandchild this time –
with thousands of others
though very few actual palms –
this twentieth time
Justice for the refugees

The African music is loud
the deep drum's vibrations
come right through the ground
and into the heart

For over a year
I have worn this valve
of titanium
but never before
have I felt
it thrum
with a drum

And suddenly to the beat
the beautiful black youth –
dreadlocked, bright-coloured –
begin their performance
with cartwheels and handstands
throwing and jigging
juggling and jiggling

solo and in groups
like brilliant sparks of a fire
as sparks not dependent on ground
but flying and dancing upwards

The six-year-old
watches entranced
announces he wants to join
the Ethiopian Circus –
but is unaware
his own vivid colouring –
red hair, blue eyes
pale pale skin –
are hardly compatible

He practices cartwheels
and handstands
all the way home
already he has learnt the trick
of the step skip
which prefigures each new movement
with the professionals.

The Ethiopian Circus
were once asylum seekers too
as were we all
That's why they are here
That's why we are here

2004 – St Petersburg Animals

It didn't dance
this little muzzled bear
clung with real affection
to its carer
master, owner, handler
Unaware
that all around the newlyweds
might pay to hold it
Fertility symbol
that it was

Also represented
where the brides flocked
beneath the statue of the Emperor
on his rearing horse
were other animals
Dogs of various breeds
Doves hidden in long boxes
An elegant black stallion
wearing red leggings
led by a girl of eight.

As three musicians
(all brass) started up
Mendelssohn's wedding march
over and over
to greet each new
bridal party

and Neptune posed
in full finery –
money changed hands
photos were taken
corks popped.
There were smiles all round.

To tourists
the street-sellers hawk
bags of tomatoes, socks (six pairs left)
and the ubiquitous
Babushka dolls all nesting.
But in the depths of the city
where tourists rarely go
is an underground pedestrian walk
lined with women
each holding
one or two subdued – drugged?
kittens for sale
Not for the tourist cameras *Nyet!*

Baby bear –
yes I held you
and paid money for the privilege.
As I stroked your coarse brown fur
and restrained your struggles
to return to your only friend
I thought,
tears in my eyes,

*Where oh where
is your mother?
And where will you go
when you've grown?*

2005 – Grandfathers

Two grandfathers apiece,
and I knew neither of mine

Grandson tips the jewellery box
out pour rings, bracelets, necklaces
last of all falls a small silver tin
with a flip-top lid – a matchbox for lucifers
belonged to my mother, belonged to her father –

Job hunting in the Depression on his bike,
knocked and killed when she was sixteen.
The matchbox was taken from his body.
For many years you could still see traces
of his actual blood.

The child's eye lights on treasure!
Two crossed swords, gold on rich blue enamel
heavy gold back engraved with mysterious words
A fine piece, rarely worn. The overt symbolism grisly
and the covert? Who knows?
Perhaps passing Masons make secret signs?
Father's father: Masonic Lodge Grand Master
irascible worthy naïve, missed me by a few years only.

Little grandson sorts through entranced
tries on a pair of blue orchid earrings
makes shapes with chains
discovers matching brooch and bracelet
lifts the lid of the matchbox, covets the swords.

He needs no memorial of an unknown grandfather –
memories of games and indulgences
kindness and care
are laid down afresh every day.

2006 – For a Cat is Good to Think On

with thanks to Christopher Smart

For every house is incomplete without me
I am the centre of the universe
Where no cat is the humans gaze at nothing
Soon I am there to fill that cat-shaped hole

I am the centre of the universe
Black marks on rustling page obscure his face
Soon I am there to fill that cat-shaped hole
Purr lovingly against his cheek and chin

Black marks on rustling page obscure his face
Nothing is sweeter than my peace at rest
Purr lovingly against his cheek and chin
Then grooming of his beard with claw and tongue

Nothing is sweeter than my peace at rest
Nor more demanding when a lap's required
Grooming of his beard with claw and tongue
The gap is filled, there's vacuum no more

Demanding when a warm lap is required
But nothing's brisker than my life in motion
The gap is filled, there's vacuum no more
Perforce that pesky carpet I'll defeat

Nothing's brisker than my life in motion
Ambush, thrash of tail – I pounce and growl
Perforce that pesky carpet I'll defeat
I'm in the house so ask to be let out

Ambush, thrash of tail – I pounce and growl
Of course I win! It's victory to me!
I'm in the house so ask to be let out
Why does he let it rain when celebration calls?

Of course I win! It's victory to me!
Where no cat is the humans gaze at nothing
I am the centre of the universe
And every house is incomplete without me

2007 – Dedication

I am dedicated to an idea.

Straight from school
studying librarianship,
I discovered my life's work.
To convince people
not to underestimate infant minds
I discovered first *Books Before Five*
A New Zealand librarian's diary
(White) of reading to her young child.

Inevitably, I also discovered Piaget
and saw the similarities as well as the differences
between the impoverished and orphaned children
he was working with and Carol White
and even with Piaget's own children
In what they were able to express
as well as how they were treated
Given the words and listened to carefully
children can understand anything
Conservation of matter, numbers
reality versus pretence, even theory of mind
Things Piaget didn't see revealed in his orphans
until they were seven or so.
They were all there in very small children

Who is to record this effect of
immersion in books but
the parents watching?
Noting games and conversations
as well as books reading and quotes.

Yes, it is 'speaking for the other' as Said
would have it, but if the studied one
is unspeaking and pre-writing
too, let alone pre-generalisation
how is the child's intelligence
and understanding ever to be recorded?

Dedication I wish I had written to the book

Stories, Pictures and Reality: Two Children Tell
To two children who have become
>delightful
>responsible
>courageous
>story-loving
>philosophical

adults, whose youthful words I have hoarded and used
to remind readers to never underestimate children's
understanding, however young.

And to their
>loving
>caring
>supportive
>knowledgeable
>philosophical

father John, without whose help and enthusiasm
this book would not exist

2008 – Bianca

As I feed
The two remaining chooks
Heavy cloud
Covers half the sky
Beneath it the sun rises
Painting the underneath cloud
Bright yellow grey

She was faithful
In her way
Laid day by day
As she should
Stood patiently
In her position
At the bottom of the pecking order
But companionable too
The youngest
And the flightiest
But a good little chook
Beautiful
Her whiteness
Part of the black/brown/white pattern
Her eggs part of the pattern, too

She'd always limped
Perhaps she carried
The root of her problem
With her always

Perhaps she faithfully
Laid her eggs
Past a tumour
But didn't seem
To be in pain

Soon afterwards
The lowering clouds
Have covered the sky
The early morning
Resounds with the sound
Of thunder
Summer storm
Marks her passing

Marks too the act
Of deliberate killing

I have never killed before
Larger than an insect or arachnid
Never a backbone
And never a flighty companion
Of half a year or more

She it was
Who refused to be caught
When taken
On a Gastronome's Tour
Of Mamma's back garden

She it was
Who caused John to wedge
In the space between
Garage and fence
One hand holding
A chook aloft
Chook back in the chook run
But would John
Be forced to stand
Sideways outside
Forever?

We tried
To treat her
With Dettol and Derris Dust
Her scratched side
Bleeding
Smelt of chicken flesh
As an uncooked carcass
On the bench
Awaiting the oven
Horrific in the living

She took so long
To trust enough
To eat from an outstretched palm
Perhaps she was right

In the end
It was that palm that took her
To an early death
But also
We hope
To a release from pain

Bianca

2009 – War Story

for Joan Eismer, 1922–2004

Fifty-six years ago
she burnt his letters.
Better, she thought,
to destroy her love
with the evidence of it
and get on with life.

So she married,
had five children –
her *rhythm quintet*.
Divorced she married again
this time with affection
and was widowed.

We, a loving couple
who have been
together for years
her neighbours and companions –
Only when it seemed
we too would be parted
by death,
only then, only then
did she dare to grieve –
for the love
she had lost so young,
for the person
she had not shared her life with,
for herself.
She cried for days.

And was left
with the ability
to recreate him.

She talks to him,
shares with him
her deepest thoughts
her slightest whims.

Elderly as he would have been.
now he is with her always.

2010 – Everything Has Meaning

With thanks to Joan London's *The Golden Age*

It was a rare moment
book group in agreement
All of us, young in the fifties, identified
But the core of the book, Frank's poetry,
the door to a world
that made everything have meaning
ignored by all but the poet
and now I expiate

Polio – everyone was at school
with someone in calipers
The once-nurses had stories to tell
of working in once-polio hospitals
so did the physios
Post-polio syndrome was discussed
but not Frank's own theory
Polio is like love. When you think
You have recovered it comes back

His reffo parents leaving
sophisticated Budapest
resonated with two members
who told us their stories
leaving Hungary;
one with rich parents
relatively easy;

one with poor parents
she a little child and cold
fled across the border
Left school at fifteen
won a uni scholarship
New Australians all.

I wonder if there is a poet
growing up here somewhere?
Poetry made Frank see the world
and the English language come alive
the modern joy of not-rhyming
sounding just the way
a person speaks –
made everything have meaning

2011 – Break-fast

A blue pottery breakfast bowl
holds muesli, fruit, milk, admiration, affection
Comes the moment
We were never close
Shards to make a mosaic.

2012 – Land/Lord

Inspired by 'How Shall I Sing the Lord's Song in a Strange Land?' choral music by Joseph Twist, inspired by Oodgeroo Noonuccal's poem 'On Hope'

The land is our parent
it owns that tree
that waterhole
that kangaroo
that mountain
that grain, that yam
and the stories belonging to them
the words for all these

The land doesn't own
these white strangers
who come from
an unimaginable place
They try to say
that it is they
who own the land
with a coloured piece
of skin on a pole
They do not know
this bush, this river,
this animal, this food
they do not know
the words for them
much less their stories

They come to teach
praise of their Lord.
They should
worship the Land
which supplies all needs
But they won't listen
they can't hear
the words to sing
the Land's song

2013 – Regrowth: Falls Creek (3 haiku)

White and lacy
Toes hidden
In frothy green petticoats

Broad stokes with a white brush
Criss-cross patterns
Across a cerulean sky

Grey-green pelt
Shot with silver
Burnt mountains regenerate

2014 – Jo's Farewell

Jo Goodman, 27.9.1940–24.7.2014

We gathered on Sunday –
authors, artists, editors, publishers,
librarians, lecturers –
the children's book people of Victoria
to farewell Jo after thirty-five years
on the Children's Book Council's
Victorian executive committee.

And farewelled her we did
in style, with a *Wild Rumpus*
in a wonderful new
school library
and a Memory Book
full of praise and admiration

Font of all knowledge
but child-like too
(soft toy Ratty her constant companion)
Caring, considerate, kindly
Firm friend to many
to whom one could turn
for advice and information
The unorthodox jewel in our crown

And she farewelled us too
Her humour, her passion
came through with inspiration
Her work on the executive
The development of RIBIT
(Read in Bed, it's Terrific)
But most of all, getting kids to read
(Who will forget young Kelly
emerging from the library
three more *Little House* books
tucked under her arm:
*I've spent so much f-ing time
reading the first one, I might as well
f-ing finish them all now!*)

We all thought we were saying goodbye
to Jo's years on the executive –
her encyclopaedic knowledge
of how the Council worked –
has always worked till last year –

moving from state to state
When it was Victoria's turn
she was on the National Executive.
Had been Victorian President
Newsletter Editor,
Victorian Judge for the
Book of the Year Awards twice –
Years of work
on the Awards Handbook
Her organisation of author/illustrator talks
Early on with the help of publishers –
Russell Hoban, Anne Fine
and Diana Wynne Jones were highlights
latterly her series of illustrators' seminars
with ZartArt have included Shaun Tan,
Margaret Wild with all her artists
Her children's book wisdom
Her articles and reviews in *Magpies*.

> We didn't know
> She didn't know
> That these were real goodbyes
> That three days later she'd be dead
> her genetically dodgy lungs
> catching up with her at last
>
> We saw her and we loved her
> being herself
> Her enthusiasm, *joie de vivre*, passion
> The Victorian doyen of children's books

Farewell Jo.

2015 – Aylan Kurdi

He lies on the beach
blue shorts, red tee.
Runners on his feet

Not asleep
though he looks it
He won't be walking
any more

Only three years old
he doesn't know he's gone viral
Too late for him
but not to help the world
find some kindness

2016 – The Truth is Out

The truth is out.
Blown out like a candle
Illumination gone
Reading has to stop
Mindless darkness stays

The truth is out:
The fire has gone quite cold
Blackened twigs and logs
Malevolently dowsed
Ashes alone remain

The truth is out;
Oh no! It has escaped
Roaming free as air
They've all set out to catch it
Searching everywhere

The truth is out:
the hand has been well trumped
the game goes on no more
the cards are on the floor
a triumphant grin remains

The truth is out:
It stumbled on the turn.
Excluded from the race
Now it trails the field
There's no way it can win

The truth is out:
Down for the final count.
It's lying on the floor
It took a knockout blow
Recovery unsure

The truth is out:
It's crying at the door
So lonely shut outside
Miserable, bedraggled
Begging to come in.

The truth is out:
>Then Trump trumped truth
>Now Truth trumps Trump
>Now there are no secrets
>NOW we understand!

2017 – Hair

Just born
My hair thick
black and curly
Bored nurses
brought me to Mother
for feeds
with hair brushed into curls
fringes, parted
an almost-page-boy
Each feed different
My Greek forebears
rejoiced

But it fell out
Replaced by blonde curls
brushed round Mother's fond finger
every morning
with the accompaniment of
Curly Pet
and her story
Anne on the Farm
continuing from day to day
A chore that
with a sibling due
Mother decided to cut
for the first time
figuratively
and physically

It grew again
now brown and wavy
usually in plaits for school
then ponytail
as was sixties fashion
Thick and lustrous
people admired
its length in the street
Not until I was fifty
was it cut short again.

Two heart operations later
it is still short
but has returned to
infant curls
rioting over the head
Yes, they are white
but – look – curly!   I'm pleased!

2018 – Moonshadows

Splinters of brightness
dazzle my eyes
as I wake
to the full moon
through the bedroom window

Moon shadows
of big battered banana leaves
inscribe my bare skin
I remember that bananas
are overgrown grass
I feel like a field mouse

Later intricate
grape leaf shadows
form a William Morris
pattern covering me
from top to toe

2019 – Thylacine

Chauvinism killed it
in Hobart Zoo
that last representative
of a whole species

Placental chauvinism –
the preference for mammals
which carry their offspring
discreetly out of sight
in a womb as do we –
So primitive
she carried a foetus
outside in her pouch
There were plenty more
where she came from:
so many that sheep farmers
insisted they needed
a bounty on their heads

Male chauvinism too
The head keeper dead
Alison his daughter
had cared for the animals
for years, paid and unpaid
No money for trained keepers
and she, a female
unable to be appointed

The zoo key was taken from her
and she listened helpless
as night after night
with cough-barks
the marsupial called her
to open the inside door
and let it into
its warm enclosure
to escape the bitterness
of the Hobart night
till it died, outside
unprotected and exposed
Chauvinism killed it

Celebrated now as Benjy
that thylacine stands in school projects
for all the Australian animals
so quickly being made extinct
by man

But the lone lonely
noble animal,
last of the great
marsupial carnivores,
was female

2020 – Old One Dicing (5 prose poems)

'I am convinced [the Old One] does not play dice with the universe'
– Einstein

Dicing with Stilled Life

The stench of ruptured guts and raw flesh was pervasive, as were the cries of terrified animals. What's going to happen to me? Indeed. *You poor things, having endured a tightly packed cattle truck, being jolted along for hours; pooed on by those above you.* Goodbye to the grass and the paddock and the dam, the open sunlight and rain showers. *You will be stunned then killed like all the others.* People will forget all this and enjoy their spaghetti bolognaise, their hamburgers, their steak and chips – with loud smacking of lips. It's not a dead animal, it's 'beef'. Disguised as a rough-clad uni student, Old One stands outside the abattoir holding a sign – *Stilled Life! This is what 60% of earth's biomass goes through for you!* Few people stop and read and ask questions – the abattoir is far off the beaten track of course. But a few stop. Will she stay and be amused by their hypocrisy, or take off to somewhere less amusing but more satisfying? She puts down the sign, digs the dice from her inside pocket, and crouches to find out.

Dicing with Reality

The camp fire, having roasted the yams and the goanna, has died down to warm embers. Old One sits beside it, beneath the stars, and holds forth. Disguised as an Elder, long white hair pulled back by a bark-band, long white beard. The adults sit around. *If only the invaders realised* he says. *Each sentient being makes their own version of the universe – reality is what they perceive, think, feel. When everyone thinks as one, they can live peacefully together for sixty thousand years. We proved that. We worship, respect, love Mother Earth and all her life-forms. But there's no escaping the parallel universes now.* He thinks of the hive mentality of termites, ants and bees, which works perfectly well, and would not destroy its wholeness, as the white invaders persist in doing to Earth. Should Old One take a break on the second planet of the star on top of the Dark Emu's head? Watch herd mentality peacefully at work? He pulls out the dice hidden in his headband and casts…

Dicing Planet B

Old One flounced into the board room batting her long eyelashes as she said *Good day gentlemen – and lady* in a gentle voice. She crossed long luscious legs with their high heels. *I've been thinking, maybe there's something we could do. Perhaps we could clean the waste water with vibration. We haven't tried that, but I've read about it working.* Unused to listening to thoughts from a female, or from a scientist for that matter, the board muttered among themselves uneasily. Two men exchanged glances and left with an *Excuse me* to discuss it in the Men's. Would they listen to the environmental experts to save the river and its load of fish? It would cost money. Help in making of this planet unsuitable for human habitation? Maybe intelligence would evolve some day from the remnants of earth-adapted living things – whales and cockroaches were standing in the wings. Old One probably wouldn't be there to find out if there was there a Planet B. Was the idea of galactic space ships full of people and culture from Earth, nothing but a pipe dream? Old One slipped two dice from her beaded bag and placed them unobtrusively on the table in front. Would she stay or go? Discover along with the hapless humans whether they would find a Planet B to wreck as well as they had done Earth? Besides, she found the unheeded-female-scientist disguise hard to keep up and boring.

Dicing with Fire

(thanks to Dorothea Mackellar)

In the city, smoke-coloured sunlight throws unexpected orange into corners of houses, flickering like flames as leaves flutter before it on the polluted air. Old One smiles at the irony. The wide brown land beckoned fifty years ago. Sun, wind and tide could be for power, rather than fossil fuel. So did their leaders lead? Work to change the climate change? To be crowned with laurel leaves as innovators? No, they built the world's biggest coal mine instead; kept accepting personal bribes from the giants; offering them grants from the public purse. *Till the sunburnt country turned to a bush-burnt country* Old One thought. *This wilful lavish land.* Hectares and hectares of native forest, uplands, downlands, burnt to a crisp. Millions of iconic animals homeless, foodless, some species gone forever. Homes lost and human lives. And the leaders lead in showing how a beleaguered country lives with climate change. Old One is here in his high-vis vest – exactly the same stomach-wrenching orange – disguised as a boilermaker and volunteer rural firey. As the team, hoses in hand, watch the fire-front crest the hill – collecting several buildings on the way – Old One squats by a cleared patch of road and fishes the dice from an inside pocket. Insectivore swarming planet Xenon awaits, and this planet is almost finished – wiped clean for a new intelligence to evolve. Will he wait out the result? Old One is curious.

Dicing with Horses

In the background stood four giant horses – Clydesdales they looked like, huge-footed, riderless. The Four Horses of the Apocalypse. They stood alert and genial. They had a job to do and were waiting to get on with it. Clearly sentient. Not enjoying the experience either, sympathetic to all. War turned to Fire and spoke in neighs clearly understood. *I don't think you'll be needed this time my dear. You worked your magic so thoroughly last year!* Fire jiggled her head up and down in acknowledgement. *Ah yes, my time is to come. It's still Plague's turn.* Old One, their groom and so-called handler, stood by with a wry smile on his face. The destruction of the top predator here on Earth proceeded apace. Soon all intelligences would have been wiped out, yet again. Old One wondered if he would wait to view the end after all or leave the Four Horses to get on with it by themselves. Famine would have the final task. *Let the dice decide as usual.* On planet Gritzel they might or might not be ready to listen to him. *Yes maybe it's time to move on.* His two trusty dice emerged from the apron pocket and spilled to the ground. Eagerly, Old One watched for the result.

2021 – My Lockdown Life

At six the alarm. No swimming or gymming – the pool is shut. I run to the toilet, weigh myself. Out to the kitchen to have a Lasix with a few mouthfuls of water, morning drops in eyes. Holed up in the study with a couple of poems to show for it, get dressed, clean teeth. Brunch (muesli, fruit and milk) at eleven thirty. Take seven morning tablets and another Lasix. Read and granny nap till three. Write in study some more (interspersed with Spider solitaire). Eight thirty to kitchen, help with tea. Outside to pick spinach leaves, Lebanese cress, Tommy tomatoes, last boysenberries – make salad. Eat dinner, sweets (yoghurt and fruit), take five evening tablets (with cold chai drink), two lots of eye drops. Close down computer. Bed with a book and husband. Midnight. One sibling, one boy, one girl, one grandchild – heaps of friends, heaps of tablets. One lovely husband, fifty years happy.

2022 – Tree Skin

They're not like us
They're not real people
Yes, they've got arms and legs
mouth and eyes
but the skin
coloured like bark!
They can't really be people

The angophoras
in their smooth pink-grey skin
lifted their limbs to the sky
joyously existing

2023 – Smells

What I smell of:
swimming pool water
hidden farts
old woman

What I can't smell:
old woman
hidden farts
swimming pool
freesias, violets
scented lilies
basil, lemon

The senses fade
Smell goes first
taking taste with it

It could be worse
I know how violets
and basil
used to smell

And I could easily
be dead
instead…

Then I couldn't smell at all
but I'd smell even worse
and be utterly unable
to immortalise in verse

Acknowledgements

These poems have been previously published on paper in the following journals, anthologies and collections.

'A Spenser Fitte' in *Lot's Wife,* 24, no. 11, 18 June 1984.

'The Juggling Librarian' in *Access,* December 1991.

'Real People' and 'Baby Walking' in *Mother Lode: Poems Reflecting on Motherhood*, ed. Jean Sietzema-Dickson. Mont Albert North, Vic.: Poetica Christi Press, c. 2003.

'Real People' in *Did I Tell You?: 131 Poems for Children in Need*, eds Nicky Gould and Vicky Wilson. Herne Bay, Kent: Categorical Books for WordAid, 2010.

'Weeaproinah' and 'Watercolour' in *The Place of Rest*, ed. Brian Edwards. Geelong: Mattoid/Grange in assoc. with Deakin University, 2013.

'Moondance' and 'For a Cat is Good to Think On' in *That Untraveled World*, ed. Brian Edwards. Geelong: Mattoid/Grange in assoc. with Deakin University, 2014.

'Aylan Kurdi' and 'Commitment?' in *Wand'ring Steps*, ed. Brian Edwards. Geelong: Mattoid/Grange in assoc. with Deakin University, 2015.

'Words and Birds' in *Poetry Without Borders* ed. by Anna Trowbridge. [n.p.] Atla Publishing [2016?]

'Introduction', 'The Company we Keep' and 'Mothering: Arboreal' in *Un-turn This Stone and Other Stories.* [n.p.] Atla Publishing [2016?]

'Mothering: Ekphrasis' in *Short and Twisted: Stories and Poems with a Twist*, ed. by Kathryn Duncan. Knoxfield, Vic.: Celapene Press, 2017.

'Love the Oxymoron' in *Poetry d'Amour 2017: Love Poems*, sel. Kevin Gillam. Inglewood: WA Poets, 2017.

'Land/Lord' in *Journal of Postcolonial Writing*, Vol. 53 no. 5, October. 2017.

'Grandfathers', 'Weeaproinah'. 'Moondance', 'Hello Yellow', 'Postcodes', 'Worlds: Creation and Demise', 'Baby Walking', 'Open Heart', 'Thylacine', 'Land/Lord' and 'Conception of a Grandmother' in *Lines Between Virginia and John Lowe*. Melb.: Melbourne Poets Union, 2018.

'Aylan Kurdi' in *This is Home: Essential Australian Poems for Children*, sel. Jackie French. Canberra: NLA Publishing, 2019.

'Dicing with Fire' in *Messages from the Embers: From Devastation to Hope, Australian Bushfire Poetry Anthology*, eds Julia Kaylock and Denise O'Hagan. Sydney: Black Quill Press, 2020.

'Cousins' and 'Footsteps' in *Poetry d'Amour 2021: Love Poems*, sel. Peter Jeffery. Perth: WA Poets, 2021.

The blog of Silver Birch Press, though not on paper, inspired with prompts a number of the autobiographical poems.

During the 1990s and 2010s onwards, my husband John and I have belonged to four poetry workshops run usually monthly by Brian Edwards, Linda Weste, Cecilia Morris and Vicky Tsaconas. Many of the poems have been immeasurably enriched by these leaders and the other poets at their groups.

www.ingramcontent.com/pod-product-compliance
Lightning Source LLC
Chambersburg PA
CBHW071452080526
44587CB00014B/2084